THE
30-DAY
MENTAL
CHALLENGE

"ALL YOU HAVE TO DO IS TRY."

MITCH HOROWITZ

MEDIA

Published 2023 by Gildan Media LLC
aka G&D Media
www.GandDmedia.com

Front cover design by Tom McKeveny

Interior design by Meghan Day Healey of Story Horse, LLC.

Library of Congress Cataloging-in-Publication Data is available upon request

ISBN: 978-1-7225-1071-8

10   9   8   7   6   5   4   3   2   1

30-Day Mental Challenge Testimonials

"Kicking off day 6 of the #30DayMentalChallenge—I always dismissed the 'positive thought' movement as something somehow beneath me, preferring complicated and arduous meditation and nuanced esoteric rituals for my own self-improvement journey. After reading *The Miracle Club* my understanding and opinion of New Thought shifted and I've been eager to try it. Six days in, and I've resumed my daily meditation practice after an unfortunate six-month lapse. I'm back to daily spiritual studies as well, and I hope to god the book is composed of every single one of these essays (at least in part) . . . These meditations have been a life-saver during a very challenging time. No lie."

"I wanted to write and share with you a truly remarkable experience that has just happened and also to thank you again . . . I am so grateful to you for your time, wisdom and support. Beginning around mid-March, I began the 30-Day Mental Challenge. I spent twice a day in deep meditation concentrating on my goal . . . Well, it was an intense experience in the best possible way and I am beyond blessed to tell you that yesterday (the last day of my challenge), I received an email letting me know that my grant proposal has been approved and they will be moving forward . . . I still can't believe it, as nothing like this has ever happened to me in my career . . . Your work has helped me overcome so many obstacles and I feel so grateful to you and your work. It truly means the world to me. Magick is real and man, it is such a beautiful, positive thing!"

"I'd like to think I know myself somewhat, but I'm also open to not having a clue and being way off the mark. I often feel the greatest challenge for me is accepting myself and thus allowing that real self to find its way out into the world authentically. Thanks for all this challenge over the past 30 days ... It has given me much to reflect upon."

"Finding one's own way that works—'the naturalness of right functioning'—is one of the most useful ideas I've encountered from your work. Unlike so many others, I never see you offering panaceas or one-size-fits-all solutions—and the practices you suggest are always offered as invitations rather than hard prescriptions. Thank you for that. After years of studying and practicing the precepts of various spiritual and self-help literature, I've sometimes felt like the more I read the less I know; not exactly true, but more reflective of trying to discover one 'true' path of trying to shoehorn a specific philosophy or ethos into my life. My confusion stemmed from thinking I should adopt other people's paths or truths *wholesale* simply because that path worked for them and some parts (or even most) of it resonated with me. The approach you suggest, finding what works for each individual (if I'm understanding you correctly), is both practical and tremendously freeing. The 'one true thing' I suppose I've discovered over the years is my aversion to dogmatic thinking and my love for pragmatism. 'But does it work for me?' is always an excellent question and seems to resolve most of my confusion. Thanks for bringing clarity and loosening some rigidity in my thinking!"

"Thank you, Mitch. It's been a great experience, and I have definite tangible results to show for it."

"This has been transformative, beyond expectation. Thank you."

"Thank you!!! For introducing this amazing opportunity to be badass at life! Day 30 yes, but after seeing the results of even transforming the not-so-important little thoughts throughout my day, I have found that it has made me feel more grateful and appreciative of life. I will continue this as I move forward. It came at a much-needed time as I am taking care of a family member who will reach end of life soon. I was so deeply sad but now I see this as an honour and an opportunity to give so much love to him. Thank you!"

"Thank you so much, Mitch. Many new life lessons learned. Can't wait for the next challenge."

CONTENTS

OPENING NOTE TO YOU

In matters of self-development, I believe strongly in the efficacy of simple methods. The key is passion and wanting. Indeed, what first looks simple often proves more complex than it appears. Profundity reveals itself in application. It is only when you attempt to *act* on an ethical or spiritual principle that its challenges appear—and you confront questions about yourself. You may also encounter extraordinary breakthroughs. In matters of the search, I believe in accelerants, which might be called epiphanies, moments of clarity, or conversion experiences.

Since this is a handbook of action, you encounter its exercise quickly. This exercise first ran in November 2015 in *Science of Mind* magazine. I have adapted it here. Based on notes from readers (some of which appear in this book) and social media responses, I estimate that thousands of people have tried it. I have also included the full testimony on which the exercise is based in Appendix A, which makes valuable reading in itself. Other appendices follow to support your efforts. They highlight the work and ideas of three of the most intriguing and underappreciated figures in the positive-mind movement: physician and scientist Richard C. Cabot (1868–1939), French mind theorist Emile Coué (1857–1926), and Australian psychiatrist and clinician Ainslie Meares (1910–1986). These are names and careers we should all know.

Following the challenge exercise, a daily meditation appears in the section *Stronger Every Day*. Read the meditations each morning, preferably as you awaken. If you have a morning meditation routine (which I recommend; my practice is Transcendental Meditation), you can read the day's passage immediately after. It is important to approach this material daily before you pick up your phone and the needs of the day pull you in. I also recommend rereading the challenge each morning and whenever you mark off a day.

Part of the power of this exercise, and my reason for publishing it in book form, is that it functions as a group effort. The meditations are adapted from a real-time 30-Day group I conducted online. Hence, I hope they convey immediacy. The meditations are designed to support everyday issues, goals, and barriers. Remember: on any given day, no matter when you start, you are embarking on this journey with like-valued seekers, often myself included, as I have repeated the challenge several times. Special potency arises from effort and exchange, which the daily meditations support.

If you encounter difficulties or setbacks during these 30 days, there is no need to start over. Just continue on. Switchbacks are natural to any road. You may also discover sudden and remarkable breakthroughs and solutions, as I and others have.

*   *   *

Although several testimonials appear at the front of this book, I want to conclude this introduction with a personal and detailed note I received in 2022 from educator Keith McNeil. It appears with Keith's permission.

> Hi Mitch,
>
> I've been meaning to email for some time to thank you for your work, which I appreciate very much. However, knowing your concern with evidence and results, I wanted to let you

know about my experiences with the 30-Day Mental Challenge. I have completed it on multiple occasions and it invariably brings results. Things go my way, I make new friends, things that were problems become opportunities and my relationships are improved. I last began the challenge on the 27th of January this year, but first a little back story.

I have worked in education as a teacher and assistant principal for the last 12 years. Although I worked in a great school with an excellent reputation, I was unhappy and disenchanted with my work for a variety of reasons (your writing about "ruling in hell" resonated strongly with me) and I was desperate for change.

I had been applying for roles without success for some time and was considering leaving education altogether. In October of 2021, an acting principal role came up at a school nearby that I knew well. I was desperate to get the job and I worked hard on my application and interviewed well. Despite all this I was unsuccessful again. I was crestfallen but filled with a new determination that I needed to move on.

With the beginning of 2022, I prepared to start applying for roles again and to aid me in this process I started the 30-Day Mental Challenge. Six days into the challenge, I was sitting in the school playground when my phone rang. It was the regional director wanting to know if I was still interested in the acting principal job that I had applied for in October, and could I start next week. The successful applicant had decided the job wasn't for them. Fast forward three months and here I am about to begin my second term as principal and having had the first part of my DCA [Definite Chief Aim] come to pass.

So, thank you Mitch for you work in bringing these ideas to the fore through your writing, It is immensely encouraging.

All the very best,
Keith

PS I forgot to mention that I have found that I feel as though the process is strengthened through carrying the written passage folded up in my pants pocket. Every time I put my hand in my pocket or brush past it, I am reminded to focus on the positive.

* * *

I trust that you will see some of your own needs and aspirations reflected in Keith's account—and that his experience gives you a sense of personal possibility during these 30 days. All you have to do is *try.*

—Mitch Horowitz

THE 30-DAY
MENTAL CHALLENGE

American philosopher William James (1842–1910) yearned to find a practical spirituality, one that produced concrete improvements in happiness.

The Harvard physician grew encouraged, especially in his final years, by his personal experiments with New Thought, which in his 1902 *The Varieties of Religious Experience* he called "the religion of healthy-mindedness." I challenge today's seekers to continue James's search for a testable, workable spiritual system. Will you attempt a 30-day experiment that puts positive-mind metaphysics to the test?

The experiment is based on a passage from a 1931 book, *Body, Mind, and Spirit* by Elwood

Worcester and Samuel McComb. The authors, both Episcopal ministers, founded the Emmanuel Movement in 1906, a respected healing ministry popular in the early twentieth century. The Emmanuel Movement was named for Emmanuel Church in Boston's Back Bay. Worcester and McComb, joint pastors of the church, drew together ministers, physicians, psychologists, and patients to study and apply the regenerative abilities of the mind. They collaborated with mainstream medical authorities, the most remarkable of which was Harvard physician and scientist Richard C. Cabot (1868–1939), who acted as Emmanuel's chief medical advisor. Cabot aimed to wed the possibilities of mind-power to scientific rationalism, and to devise a mental therapeutics that could win allies among medical authorities.*

In *Body, Mind, and Spirit*, a prominent scientist, who the authors did not name, told a small audience how he radically improved his life through a one-month thought experiment. I have condensed his testimony:

---

* I encourage reading more deeply into the Emmanuel Movement not only from a historical but also a practical perspective. Understanding Emmanuel's efforts will contribute to your success with the 30-day experiment. Appendix B is a historical portrait of Cabot, Emmanuel's most impressive exponent, and the movement in general.

Up to my fiftieth year I was unhappy, ineffective, and obscure. I had read some New Thought literature and some statements of William James on directing one's attention to what is good and useful and ignoring the rest. Such ideas seemed like bunk—but feeling that life was intolerable I determined to subject them to a month-long test.

During this time, I resolved to impose definite restrictions on my thoughts. In thinking of the past, I would dwell only on its pleasing incidents. In thinking of the present, I would direct attention to its desirable elements. In thinking of the future, I would regard every worthy and possible ambition as within reach.

I threw myself into this experiment. I was soon surprised to feel happy and contented. But the outward changes astonished me more. I deeply craved the recognition of certain eminent men. The foremost of these wrote me, out of the blue, inviting me to become his assistant. All my books were published. My colleagues grew helpful and cooperative.

*It seems that I stumbled upon a path of life, and set forces working for me which were previously working against me.**

*   *   *

Let's repeat this experiment together: 1) Choose your start date, 2) write out the full italicized, quoted passage above by hand (never underestimate the value of that), and 3) add: "I dedicate myself on this day of _____ to focus on all that is nourishing, advancing, and promising for thirty days (signed) _____ "

That's it.

I suggest writing this passage on an index card and on the reverse creating a grid in which you mark off each of your thirty days. I advise rereading the scientist's testimony each morning and each time you mark off a day, as well as whenever it feels necessary. Another method is to write out your statement in this book itself so that you keep it at hand for daily reference. I have left space at the back, labeled *My 30-Day Mental Challenge*, for you to do so. You may want to carry this book, and your statement, with you during the day.

---

* Although it is not necessary for this experiment, I have provided the full text of the scientist's statement in Appendix A. It makes enthralling reading.

Whenever you catch yourself sliding into old habits of thought, do not worry; simply steer back to the experiment. *You do not need to start over.* Just carry on. The following 30 days of meditations are there to help you on your way.

STRONGER EVERY DAY

MEDITATIONS ON THE 30-DAY MENTAL CHALLENGE

Welcome to Day 1. To address a few common questions: 1) You need only hand copy the *quoted and italicized* passage and your pledge. Sign and date it. If you want a visual example, a photograph of one of my handwritten 30-day pledges appears in the meditation accompanying Day 9. 2) Do not worry about slips. They are wholly natural and necessary. If you don't slip you aren't doing it for real. Don't get hung up—just keep going. This is not a "mental diet" where you need to start over. 3) Positive Mental Attitude, or PMA, doesn't mean not caring. Live your life out loud—but with determinative thinking. In my estimation, PMA is not a rosy outlook but estimating events based on their *capacity for self-development.* For these 30 days we don't drift; we endeavor to determine our mentality. And to fight for what's right, including the dignity of others and ourselves. Nothing is worth more than dignity. It brings happiness when other rewards dissipate. 4) Regarding the past: we've all suffered. These 30 days are dedicated to focusing on what is advancing and productive. A great teacher once observed: "The past controls the future but the present controls the past." These 30 days are, in a sense, a redemption of the past and its struggles. They refine you. "Opposition is true Friendship," wrote William Blake in 1790 in *The Marriage of Heaven and Hell*. In a similar vein Fredrich Nietzsche wrote: *"Out of life's school of war*: what doesn't destroy me makes me stronger."* Struggle is also a payment of debt to those who have suffered on our behalf, including ancestors who labored to bring us a better life. 5) Regarding the future, you are to consider every reasonable wish as within reach. Every earned attainment is sacred—as is power that accrues to you. True power is ethical, by which I mean reciprocal. Power without ethics is force. It is unrenewable. And we are about power.

---

* *Twilight of the Idols* (1889), translated by Walter Kaufmann (1954).

What do you want from your search? This is the same as asking what you want out of life. I began this book with several testimonials—lots more could have been included—because I want to instill in you the *justified confidence* that the 30-Day Mental Challenge works. As such, you should begin this journey with a sense of hopeful expectancy. Not only that, but also with an abiding drive to direct your thoughts to the "desirable elements" referenced in the pledge. At times this will prove difficult. In moments it may prove impossible. There will be slipups. No matter. Continue on. You will be moved to do so because of the assurance that *you will find something*. Allow this warranted belief to feed your morale. No spiritual, ethical, or therapeutic philosophy or technique deserves a hold on you unless it produces concrete results, measurable in experience and conduct. We err on the path when we eschew, devalue, or redirect questions of result. We are in this for results. Indeed, you may see a special result early on. That is not to be regarded as "confirmation bias" (an overused term for prejudice) or happenstance. It is testimony and effort.

WHEN HABIT IS A BARRIER

The chief barrier facing us during these 30 days is habit. Habit is neither good or bad in itself but is self-conditioned or automatized behavior that can feel as palpable and needful as drawing breath. There are habitual dimensions to negative emotions. Watch carefully for how you derive a subtle sense of thrill, relief, or excitement from anger and resentment. These emotions and their attendant bodily effects can be addictive. Expressing anger, resentment, or bitterness can feel like a release. It can feel euphoric. We often derive unacknowledged pleasure from things that we claim to want to be rid of. This forms part of their hold on us. We frequently harbor the misleading notion that we can dilute private suffering by continually expressing it, as well as through inner talking. Philosopher William James offered a different possibility. James observed that the *assumption of a mood*, even in a seemingly superficial manner, often precipitates the resultant feeling state.* Hence, by acting "as though" you may at times discover yourself capable of reversing the polarity of negative emotions—versus continually reviewing or justifying them, or chronically (and often futilely) searching for an antecedent. Our aim today is to act "as though." Assume the state you wish to occupy.

---

* My friend Norman E. Rosenthal, M.D., a clinical professor of psychiatry at Georgetown University School of Medicine, worked with a colleague to put this thesis to the test in an unusual experiment on the effects of Botox on facial muscles. I encourage exploration of their efforts at "Don't Worry, Get Botox" by Richard A. Friedman, *New York Times*, March 21, 2014.

DAY 4
SUSTAIN PARADOX

Today's theme is paradox. Embrace it. One of the key markers of maturity on the spiritual and ethical path is the ability to sustain paradox. There is no "one ingredient" or magic pill that delivers us. (Or, if you discover such a method, I applaud it.) Sometimes, in fact, we are drawn in directions that appear divergent. That is natural. Do not feel compelled to sync every act or to explain contradictions, either within or without. Our 30-Day Mental Challenge deals with both psyche (a compact of thought and emotion) and focus. *But I also believe ardently in outward action*, especially as it involves your safety and wellbeing. I consider it a nonnegotiable imperative to *get away from cruel people*, something I often insist on. "Isn't every solution within us?" some ask. Life is a whole and its requirements are myriad. Sometimes needs that appear polarized are simply life expressing itself—and you expressing yourself. With love to Allen Ginsberg, I saw the best minds of my generation destroyed by *seeking consistency*. There's no precise ingredient to your freedom: people get caught in knots saying, "I must do it like Neville" or "like Alan Watts," and so on. No sooner will you find a way than you meet with some crossroads or barrier that sends you retracing your steps, certain that you missed something. Do not be concerned: there is a point at which paradox must be embraced. Paradox does not require fixing. *Tao Te Ching*: " The truest sayings are paradoxical."*

---

* Chapter VII, translation by Lionel Giles, 1905.

DAY 5
HARD NECESSITY

We are invested in development and not in what is always easy, steady, and familiar. Without friction there can be no refinement. Keep Eden—I'll take the road of hard necessity. Today's effort is to renew our focus with total commitment. When dwelling on the past, think only of what proved fortifying and advancing. When thinking of the present, aim your focus on progressive, productive elements. When thinking of the future, consider every reasonable aim within reach. Remember: change one element and you change everything. That is at the heart of what is called "chaos theory" (and also the root of "chaos magick"). That truth reflects life's symbiosis. You possess greater power than you realize.

DAY 6
D-DAY APPROACH

I hope today proves clarifying because I want to make a point that often gets lost in the culture of New Age, recovery, and alternative spirituality. There is no schism—at least in this program—between the spiritual search and prescription drugs (or other kinds) and varying modalities of treatment, whether traditional or alternative. I believe in availing yourself of all devices that authentically help. To summarily reject a pill or any "mainstream" treatment is to possibly neglect a doorway that may provide unforeseen assistance. I want to be clear about this: I take a daily SNRI. It isn't for everyone. But it's a help to me. I trust you to make informed decisions about your own needs. Without anyone else's politics or schooling. I write this because a know-it-all righteousness emerges in some precincts of New Age culture (no different from any other subculture); sometimes an Rx or some such is considered "cheating" or corrupt. As I often tell philosophical materialists: being right about one part of the puzzle does not mean you've figured out the whole. Certainty often proves a barrier. Instead, I endorse a "D-Day" approach to self-development: use everything available, including meditation, prayer, affirmation, visualization, therapy, yoga, cognitive tools, spell work, magick, etc.—and medicine or entheogens according to your own needs and informed decisions. "One Law for the Lion & Ox is Oppression," William Blake further wrote in *The Marriage of Heaven and Hell* in 1790. That's our principle for today.

DAY 7
OPPOSITION WITHIN

A reader asked: "How do I deal with tormenting mental voices that reassert themselves even after a good start?" The most difficult part of tormenting voices is that they arise unexpectedly. If you're like me, you're on a ladder changing a light bulb and suddenly a mental association hits and you're thinking about an old (or projected) sorrow or loss. When your personhood feels threatened, no amount of rational thought can wholly counter the resulting emotion. Emotion is more powerful than thought. Emotion is also *faster* than thought, which is why we often fail to think of rejoinders in personal confrontations, at least until after the fact. I suggest this: most of us are more anguished over *self-integrity* than what has or may happen to us. You can put up with a lot of disappointment. You cannot put up with a violation of self. We must feel that we stand for something as defined by our values, self-respect, and expressiveness. Hence, when thoughts of opposition, hurt, fear, or anger rush in—as they will and must—I suggest vowing internally, even if you don't feel it at first, that this *opposition will refine, fortify, and ennoble you* to the greatest extent possible and abet your standing taller in your inviolate self. The impulse of valor, such as in protecting self or another, is itself an emotion. This emotion can be pitted against a clouding or negative one. One act of valor, fully experienced, can alter your entire life. How, when, and where you will be summoned to that act is an open question. Suffering prepares you for that hour. Which could occur today. Do not fear life's "school of war" as Nietzsche phrased it. Let opposition serve as a goad.

DAY 8
STRONGER EVERY DAY

I am often asked for a favorite affirmation or meditation. These things are very individualized.
But I want to say something about the uses of
affirmations. First, I don't think it matters whether
you structure an affirmation in present or future
tense—don't concern yourself with structure
so long as the statement is emotionally persua-
sive to you. With that in place, there's no wrong
way. Then there is the question of use. I follow
the method prescribed by French mind theorist
Emile Coué, author of the famous mantra, "Day
by day, in every way, I am getting better and better."* Coué was shrewder and more foresightful
than is often appreciated. He prescribed using his
or any mantra in the moments before drifting to

---

* You can read further about Coué and his method in Appendix C: "The
Man Who Helped The Beatles Admit It's Getting Better."

STRONGER EVERY DAY					37

sleep at night and waking in the morning. This finds you in a state of deep relaxation and hence more open to suggestion. Sleep researchers call it hypnagogia. I use this naturally hypnotic period twice daily to gently recite mantras, affirmations, or prayers. Now, there are times when we wish to recite a self-affirming meditation and we just do not feel it. Does recitation then become a depleting self-deception? No. Even when you don't feel it, recite your affirmation. Recite it as much as possible and whenever you wish. There is an act of self-resolve in stating an ideal. It is never wrong. Over time, the repetition serves to tone your psyche, however subtly. Affirmation is not a denial of reality—nothing in these 30 days prescribes looking away from hard truths, whether social or personal—it is the statement of an ideal. "I am captain of my soul" poet William Ernest Henley wrote privately in "Invictus" in 1875 (it was not published until 1888). We live in a cynical age. One side of the culture derides affirmations as woo-woo silliness. Another side embraces idealistic statements yet sometimes behaves with unaccountability. Dispense with both ends of that stick. We are unafraid of being out of step. Assert the song of self.

DAY 9
"A PATH OF LIFE"

Monday, Nov. 9, 2020

"Up to my 50th year, I was unhappy, ineffective and obscure. I had
read some New Thought literature and
some statements of William James on
directing one's attention to what is good
and useful and ignoring the rest. Such
ideas seemed like bunk, but feeling
that life was intolerable, I determined
to subject them to a month-long test.

"During this time, I resolved to impose
definite restrictions on my thoughts. In
thinking of the past, I would dwell only
on its pleasing incidents. In thinking
of the present, I would direct attention
to its desirable elements. In thinking
of the future, I would regard every
worthy and possible ambition as within
reach.

"I threw myself into this experiment.
I was soon surprised to feel happy and
contented. But the outward changes
astonished me more. I deeply craved the
recognition of certain eminent men.
The foremost of these wrote me, out
of the blue, inviting me to become his

Many readers have shared their handwritten 30-day pledges, which are wonderful to see. Today I am sharing mine. "I stumbled on a path of life ..." Let today's theme be *back to basics*. Let's all reread our statements and recommit to the simple, powerful tool of directing our thoughts to what is advancing, productive, and fortifying. To facilitate this, any who are interested are invited to join me or others today at 3 pm eastern to silently

assistant. All my books were published. My colleagues grew helpful and cooperative.

"It seems that I stumbled upon a path of life, and set forces working for me which were previously working against me."

I dedicate myself on this day of November 9, 2020, to focus on all that is nourishing, advancing, and promising for 30 days.

reread their statement. (I am in silent affirmation each day at this time, something I write about in *The Miracle Club*.) Hold a wish of support for each other at that hour, whatever locale or time zone you're in.

Ralph Waldo Emerson observed in his 1841 essay "Compensation" (which I reread at least once a year) that we often look back on the difficulties of the past with a kind of serenity—relieved that certain challenges are safely tucked into prior years and that we successfully emerged from them, frequently with benefit and refinement. This act may be more than just memory: it may be creation. The philosophy of Neville Goddard was described to me as "remembering from the future" (thank you Duncan Trussell). This framing captures one of Neville's key methods, which is to "remember when" you occupied a lesser or more difficult state in order to *feel in the current satisfaction of having emerged from that chrysalis to something greater.* Since, as you've noticed by now, no act of mental resolve fully halts negative thoughts or emotions, I ask you today to regard those associations as *memories* in the fashion of this exercise. "Live from the end"—see these associations as barriers that you have surpassed, as steppingstones to the place you are *now* as you wish to be. Memory creates.

AGAINST PASSIVITY

What is "positive thinking?" I eschew terms like "manifestation" and "Law of Attraction" (rather, I refer to "selection" and the existence of numerous laws and forces.) But I hang onto this "golden oldie" of *positive thinking*. I like its vintage, I like its plainness—and something more. To me, positive thinking means *deliberative thinking*. It means constructive, directed, and determined thought. It does not mean a rosy or myopic outlook. It does not necessarily mean loving of neighbor or enemy or denying of opposition or evil. (In terms of the psyche, I define evil as spite.) Positive thinking does not deny concepts like victory—when pursued with reciprocity. Positive thinking does not preclude, and indeed requires, action. It directs you to keep your word. Mind-body teacher Moshe Feldenkrais (1904–1984) taught that you should be able to write down at least three solutions to any problem. Do that today. Drifting into defeatism and repetitive patterns is negative. It is the absence of new thought in favor of passivity. "Redeem defeat by new thought," wrote Ralph Waldo Emerson in his 1870 essay, "Success."

BEYOND THE GIVEN

Many readers have contacted me with moving stories—we're doing this seeker to seeker and it's important to exchange—and also with grueling challenges. I often say that we experience many laws and forces, including those of physical limitation. As noted earlier, this is why I eschew the term "Law of Attraction." I reject the implication that we live under one mental super law. While consciousness may be (and I believe is) the ultimate arbiter of reality, we do not, the vast majority of the time, dwell in that sphere alone. Kick a rock and you will feel mass—and pain. This is as much a law as any other. Yet we also dwell within the extraordinary. The mind is the medium for experience that exceeds the boundaries of the given. In *The Miracle Club*, I write about (and source) the success of placebo surgeries. This is not fantasy. I write about the precious and extremely rare but real questions of spontaneous remissions of cancer—you can read about this and review the sources in Appendix D, "How to Talk About Contentious Issues In Science." We are adults—we can search together without falling into the childish, rah-rah tone of many metaphysical churches or the binary anti-intellectualism of polemical skepticism. Today we approach the miraculous—do not fear that word—with our eyes open. Consider all possibilities within reach. The Talmudic book *Ethics of the Fathers* teaches: "Let your works exceed your wisdom." This can be read many ways. For this day, I ask you to take it to mean allowing yourself to experiment with ultimate possibilities of thought and expansion beyond the given.

THE LAW OF PERSISTENCE

Without an unmet need we would remain inert. In his magisterial *Meetings with Remarkable Men*, spiritual teacher G.I. Gurdjieff included an addendum, "The Material Question." He recounted how he and a group of students fled the Russian Revolution and found themselves desperately without money in Constantinople. They tried and tried to procure resources but their efforts failed. Just at the moment when everything seemed about to collapse, a long-forgotten resource was discovered. The group was saved. There was, the teacher concluded, something lawful in this. Gurdjieff called it "the law-conformable result of a man's unflinching perseverance in bringing all his manifestations into accordance with the principles he has consciously set himself in life for the attainment of a definite aim."* Today's principle: TRY. Both within and without. "I will not cease from Mental Fight," wrote William Blake in his 1810 ode, "Jerusalem."

---

* I consider the episode in detail in *Daydream Believer*, chapter eight, "The Wish Machine."

HARD PROOF OVER HALLOWED PRINCIPLE

D o you know what would make you happy? I ask because your life may hinge on that question, which belongs to you alone. It seems so simple. But only in appearance. We are conditioned to use words and markers in place of experience. Today, choose hard-won experience over concept. Trust your experience. When I was 12 years old and riddled with anxieties (for which I was hospitalized), I thought to myself: "If I could just go to bed and wake up feeling contented, I'd be happy." A spiritual teacher I admire said the same thing. But I no longer feel that way. Much later in life, I was flying home from a vacation (save us from vacations) and felt burdened, anxious, and depressed. I got an email from an NPR producer asking me to be on a show the next day to discuss miracles and sainthood. I went home and threw myself into research. As I did, my entire gait, mood, and outlook changed. I was happy. Just a psychological sugar high? A temporary bauble? Air through the wind chimes? No. Truth. It was at that moment that I realized what I was really supposed to be doing in life: public engagement with metaphysical topics. (And I never do anything unprepared). That amounted to real happiness for me. I tested that thesis for years and found it true. But in an instant a divine would've taken it from me—would've told me "it's the finger pointing at the moon" or some such. I say: verify. Hard proof over hallowed principle (and what we call principle is often just repetition of translated ideas). A historically venerated mystic once said that you discover the "soul" (without defining soul) not by addition but by subtraction. That is the kind of statement I once would've repeated. No longer. You discover your selfhood through a process exclusive to you. Recall the earlier statement by William Blake: "One Law for the Lion & Ox is Oppression" Again: what makes you happy? The answer is private. Find out. Test

it. The adjoining pic is of a Dead Kennedys but-
ton on my backpack, which got oxidized from my
biking in a crazy rainstorm. We're taught to avoid
the rain. But that, too, was happy.

DAY 15
REDEDICATION

Today, our midpoint, is as simple as it is radical: Rededicate yourself to reading your vow and committing to its highest fulfillment. Pause and make that commitment right now. Those of us doing this challenge are part of a community of experiment and search. I ask simply that each of us today hold the highest wishes of support for one another's efforts—and our own.

How do you conceptualize yourself? While it is true that we all have our natural aptitudes, affinities, and areas of relative strengths and weaknesses, the narrative that we self-condition plays a seismic role not only in self-perception but in determining the nature of experience. As alluded, William James observed that act often precedes and determines mood, not vice versa. In every possible instance, assume the gait of construction: frame yourself in the strongest possible terms. That act itself—even if beginning as an inner movement—will influence self-perception over time. And sometimes in remarkable ways, even within the space of a moment. This is our experiment for today. "I stumbled upon a path of life . . ."

DAY 17
HETERODOXY

Today's focus is based on "Habit 13" from *The Miracle Habits*. Few things are more depleting of your happiness and sense of self than *internalized conformity*. I do not exactly mean outer peer pressure but rather the limitations that we internalize as a matter of rote and thus limit our sense of solutions, possibilities, and avenues for self-expression. I do not suggest a go-it-alone approach to life. We are all connected and relationships are at the basis of everything. But you will naturally attract more of the people with whom you want to be connected when you stop acting "like them" and ask yourself: what do I truly want? In that vein, it is better to be nobly alone than in compromised company. The right people are drawn to you to fulfill something in themselves not to enforce something in you. Take this day, in however small a manner, to enact something constructive with no reference other than your own proclivities or passions. This might mean ridding yourself of some object—or relationship. It might mean performing a task without anyone else's approbation. It might mean rejecting an unsatisfying social or professional obligation. You will also have to shoulder the consequences and potential debt, so be thoughtful—but *be*. See how you stand afterward.

DAY 18
SILENCE IS FREEDOM

If you are following this challenge, you likely feel unsatisfied with status quo norms. For this reason, holidays or large gatherings may seem perpetually unsettling. Holidays or gatherings of workmates, friends, or family can be difficult for sensitive people. You may feel misunderstood by peers or relatives. That's because you often *are* misunderstood. Who knows us less well than our birth families? Who knows us less well than aunts and uncles and so on who want us to be like them? Or to think like them? This is true even of friends who may, through subtle putdowns and power plays, enforce roles that make you feel uneasy or unseen. If you're around such people today, my message is: you are free. You owe them no explanations, justifications, arguments or debates. When Uncle Mike starts blathering about something that you find abhorrent, you owe him . . . *silence*. Debate settles nothing. It is a form of imprisonment. Reject it. Your fealty is owed to your own freedom, selections, and wellbeing. No one—no one—has a right to bother you. If they do, walk away. Refuse to reply. If you must, just leave. Really. Like that. No games today. People will be civil to you—or they will not be in relationship to you. Is that positive? Yes. Because it's active. We are not selling syrup. We are purchasing freedom. The fee of freedom is rejection of rote thought patterns and behaviors.

DAY 19
OVERCOME RESISTANCE

I wrote earlier about the efficacy of using a mantra or affirmation during hypnagogia, an exquisitely relaxed and suggestive state experienced just before drifting to sleep and again upon waking. French mind theorist Emile Coué had an early instinct for this, later validated by sleep researchers. Scholarly psychical researchers have also found hypnagogia a period of heightened ESP, so there is a metaphysical dimension to this as well. (I write about this in *Daydream Believer.*) As noted, I also believe that there is benefit in steadfastly repeating an affirmation to yourself. Some have argued that the rational mind pushes back against unpersuasive affirmations. The rational mind rejects a lot of things, sometimes helpfully. Yet through repetition we also overcome a lot that is rational, at times to our detriment. Why not do all that is possible to reverse the process of negative self-conditioning? Neville Goddard: "An assumption, though false, if persisted in eventually hardens into fact." Let this truth be your sword and shield.

DAY 20
HONOR THE UNEXPECTED

Today I want you to feel exquisitely free to seek your good (by which I mean selfhood) anywhere. Watch carefully for the arrival of your good from overlooked sources. In ancient myths, gods, angels, or messengers are often disguised as wandering strangers. Are you neglecting a solution because it doesn't seem to belong to your conditional menu? Reject nothing out of hand. Your deliverance may arrive in a treatment, act, choice, relationship, procedure, or item that you may not anticipate. "Good things always arrive unexpectedly," said Rebbe Menachem Schneerson (1902–1994). The Rebbe said these words to Talmudic scholar Adin Steinsaltz (1937–2020) who showed up at one of his talks unannounced. We frequently hem ourselves into thinking not only in terms of our mind's eye image but also in terms of what options are available to "spiritual" people. Often this is nothing but internalized conformity: personally unverified ideas hallowed by repetition and decisions made by others. Just as problems often have a complexity of causes, solutions arrive in a complexity of ways.

DAY 21
HOW TO STAY "ON"

═══════════════════════════════════════

Today begins our final 10 days. Some readers have asked how to stay "on" the program. The truth is: if you're not falling off, you're not really doing it. Our minds and emotions—the amalgam I call our psyche—are enormously conditioned toward fear, hostility, and anger. These things are by no means *always* negative. Fear or even anger in the face of legitimate danger may be preserving. But, as in the case of PTSD, these reactions become hyper-conditioned, habitual, and automatic. Hence, such reactions perpetuate the danger that they seek to ameliorate. This is the psychological mechanism at the back of the classical Oedipus drama, whereby a dreaded prophecy is self-induced. Overcompensation for perceived flaws often proves the very thing that leads to destruction. It is perhaps the core tragedy of human nature. How much greater is that truth if, as I surmise, our minds possess causative qualities, which interplay with other forces around us? Hence, our 30-Day Challenge is not about unrealistic expectations but rather about noticing and disrupting *calcified reactions*. It is also about results. Your signed pledge references results. Have you experienced them? I believe in a results-oriented spirituality. I reject efforts to deny the demand for results or to respond to it with a corrective question. Is hunger for results a mistake, as treated in some spiritual quarters, or is it a legitimate driving factor in your efforts? In my experience, it is the latter. Allow that hunger to aid your efforts to stay "on."

IT'S ALL ONE THING

I break with a conviction of most spiritual practice: I do not believe or think in terms of "inner" or "outer" worlds or aspects of self (although I occasionally use such terms as generalities). I consider that a formula for frustration and self-negation, especially as it is acted upon in our contemporary spiritual culture. Life is a whole. Demands are a whole. Efforts are a whole. At this point in my search, I do not abide concepts of "just being," "nonidentification," "effortless effort" (although I recognize the naturalness of alignment), or "inner peace" as aids to the search for selfhood. I believe these things can tear the seeker apart, impelling us in practice to deny or needlessly condition aspiration, generativeness, and productivity. In that vein, revisit the passage from Day 13, "The Law of Persistence." The language of nonattachment is so conceptually perva-sive in our spiritual culture that it can be difficult to imagine that such ideas are not suited to my search. But this is mine—and yours—to verify.

DAY 23
WHAT IS REALITY?

Is mind the ultimate reality? I consider that modernism's most tantalizing question. (I touch on it in Day 12, "Beyond the Given.") The theme of modernist philosophy is the primacy of hidden antecedents, e.g., trauma, social class, evolution. Ninety years of data from quantum theory—and resisted but no less evidentiary data from academic ESP research—have placed us before the question of mind or perception as determinant. Quantum theory requires acknowledgment that perspective and decision (in this case, decision to take a measurement even via an automatized device) determine when or whether a subatomic particle will localize in a given place. Before a measurement, a particle occupies a place of infinitude. It is "there" only in *potential*, further necessitating the acceptance of multiple worlds and coexisting realities. That is further why I speak of "selection" versus "manifestation." Even if I generalize from this material (and I do) it must also be acknowledged that . . . we suffer. We experience physical decline. We hit limits. In short, we experience many laws and forces. In these 23 days, for example, you've probably discovered, as I've suggested, that emotions prove stronger than thoughts. Thought alone cannot curb emotion. But thought, for all its limits, is the one medium where, to paraphrase a certain hero of mine, "we reign supreme." And on the scale of the psyche, what are limits but *goads to strength*? Take today's journey knowing that forces may be aligned against your empire of mind—*yet barriers can also suddenly fall*. Especially with extraordinary effort. That's my wish for you today.

DAY 24
REJECT FORMULA

Recent to this writing, I rewatched *The Wizard of Oz* (and the remarkably underrated *Return to Oz*). I smiled at the original's reference to getting "in tune with the infinite."* That's the title of a hugely popular 1897 New Thought book by Ralph Waldo Trine. It was, perhaps, the first mass bestseller of spiritual self-help. I love what is called New Thought because I believe in its basic premise of mind causation. I have deep differences, however, with how most New Thought literature has approached suffering, hate, tragedy, oppression, and anger. There is, I believe, too

---

* In one of my favorite scenes, Dorothy is running away from home and happens upon the wagon of Professor Marvel who invites her into his fortunetelling parlor. Seating Dorothy before a crystal ball, Professor Marvel tells her: "Now, you—you'd better close your eyes, my child, for a moment—in order to be better in tune with the infinite." Neither the scene nor phrase appears in Theosophist L. Frank Baum's 1900 novel, *The Wonderful Wizard of Oz*.

much namby-pamby denialism in traditional New Thought. In the same way that certain Eastern philosophies, or their adaptations in the West, can self-divide seekers with injunctions to "nonattachment," so can America's homegrown metaphysics place an unnatural demand on the individual to see good in place of evil. Does denial of evil help the individual? Within many New Age and New Thought settings I often detect, as you might, an enormity of repressed anger, passive-aggression, self-service, and syrupy talk with concealed shivs at the ready. (A New Age magazine once broke a financial commitment to me and responded by asking that I "have compassion for the accounting department.") On a personal scale—and I cannot imagine my experience is exceptional—I find denial of friction or automatic assumptions of forgiveness depleting and unnatural. Name an animal that doesn't hiss or growl when threatened. How do we approach such issues within the framework of constructive positivity to which these 30 days are dedicated? Revisiting our theme from Day 11, "Against Passivity," I see positive thinking as the opposing polarity of inertia. Positivity is deliberateness. Positivity means eschewing the habitual and insidiously enjoyable pattern of mentally replaying grudges, a weakness with which I struggle. It means finding resolution on terms that you authentically deem reparative. It means desistance from trash talk, rumor, and gossip. *It means, finally, evaluating difficult events not through a gauzy tint but based on their capacity for self-development.* We do not seek or wish for convenience or ease but rather self-expression and expansion. You are a mature being. You must walk this road without formulaic models. Feel free to throw away sweet quotations and ask yourself: what path is active and reparative, not passive and repetitive? Let that be our effort today.

HOW TO BE POWERFUL

Life deals us a difficult but transcendent truth, which is that your greatness lies in a single direction. In his 1860 essay "Power," Ralph Waldo Emerson wrote that the formula for personal power is "concentration" and "drilling"—that is, focus on a single point and continual practice or effort in its direction. We witness this in nature: dispersal brings weakness and concentration brings force; it is the difference between water mist and a waterfall, a photon and a laser. I believe well-roundedness is overrated. The difficulty is that life demands multiple roles of us. We are employees, artists, caregivers, parents, spouses, etc., in any variegated combination. What to do? My gambit—and ours today—is that one well-selected aim, passion, or destiny (you have one) covers diffuse bases. Resources derived from one role can be dedicated to another. Barring some overwhelming countervailing force, like a severe health crisis (which is not defeat but justly requires your consuming attention), I do not think nature has presented us an untenable bargain. What is your destined aim? Do not fear or flee the portent of that question. Let that be our experiment today.

CYCLES

D ramatist and philosopher Johann Wolfgang von Goethe (1749–1832) observed in his journals that days tend to go in cycles. I have found this true. Life is rhythmical. He also observed, as Emerson paraphrased in his 1860 essay "Fate," that what you wish for when you're very young comes upon you in waves when you're old—so be careful. Is that also true? I ask you today to probe your earliest conscious memories, from ages three or four, and make that consideration. I think—barring extreme countervailing events—life evinces greater symmetry than we allow. We sometimes reject or fight this symmetry, which can leave us feeling painfully divided. There is relief, too, within symmetry. Life visits seasonal changes upon us. It sometimes exacts prices in exchange for great possibilities. Look for a compelling example of this in your experience. I write in *Daydream Believer*:

> Some social scientists (and, more often, science journalists and bloggers) label virtually any personal effort to observe connections between self and the world by the brutally compact term—at once naïve and cynical—confirmation bias. As noted, this is a clinical term for prejudice. We all suffer from it. But to overapply such a judgment to the individual search means limiting questions of emotional and ethical existence to the structures of credentialed study. The overuse of such concepts also means subtly (and futilely) attempting to upend the ageless imperative to *know oneself* in favor of professionally determined protocols of perception. It means indirectly claiming that self-inquiry is illusory outside of licensed probity. From Lao Tzu to Proust to Plath, all is, strictly speaking, mere anecdote, of no greater application to the truth of the human situation than the elections of a subject responding to forced-choice survey questions in a lab or marketing study.

When considering the question of cycles, bear in mind that near-term disappointments may be unimportant of themselves but reveal a pattern that moved you in a restorative direction. Without cycles of difficulty and deliverance, we would stagnate. We would be kept beings and not rough and free beings. Cycles are necessity.

DAY 27
WHAT DO YOU WANT?

I've written before that knowing what you want is more difficult than it may first appear. Peer culture often takes from us the capacity to self-disclose our wishes. We internalize values and decisions that belong to others. I have witnessed others (and myself) get torn apart by divided fealties or rather divisions between what we *say* we want and what we *really* want. For example, do you want people to relate to you in a certain way? Whatever that means to you, it may be entirely valid; it may not be a psychological construct but a *legitimate wish*. I think we throw away or deny our desires too easily. I have a family member who harmed herself through division and lack of self-acknowledgment. She wanted all the warmth and accolades of being in a large family—social gatherings, holiday cards, etc.—but she wouldn't lift a finger to help another person. She often caused frictions and reveled in the fallout. She was divided. She could never acknowledge that to herself. Hence, she received ersatz versions of family warmth, engendered hostility, and is now alone. Was there a better way to live? Maybe. It might have involved getting into the guts of what she really wanted (which was known to her alone). As I've often noted, including during these meditations, in terms of the psyche there is no good and evil—there is empathy and spite. Human reciprocity exists on that scale. That is my attempted code of honor. Beyond that, I ask you to consider: What is life-giving to you? What do you really want? What are you willing to sacrifice for it? That, in my estimation, is self-determined thinking.

DAY 28
DEFAULTS

I was inspired by something posted on social media by a 30-Day Challenge participant: "Day 1 of the #30daymentalchallenge was a success! Mainly just made me aware of how shockingly often my mind defaults to seeing the negative sides of life . . . It's been so much more powerful than I could have imagined. I'm struck by the fact that, prior to the last few days, I let all these negative thoughts just run rampant, unopposed in my mind. It's challenging, to be sure, but viewing it as mental calisthenics is helping . . . Anxiety and general feelings of being overwhelmed is one of my main mental hurdles. But now I notice when I'm in an anxious loop, I counter the overwhelmed feeling with excitement ('How incredible it is that I have so many projects/interests!') and just keep moving forward." Part of the premise of this exercise is that thoughts are causative. If that is so, then the sustained act of mental focus changes things; we see physical proof of this in the field of neuroplasticity, which uses brain scans to demonstrate how habitual thought alters neural pathways. I have three suggestions for today: 1) Select a book of classic New Thought literature and see how it speaks to you. Forget the snobs: I believe that popular metaphysical literature contains rejected stones. As I write these words, I am reading the 1950 book *You, Too, Can Be Prosperous* by Robert A. Russell. 2) If Abrahamic iterations of the term God are not for you, when you encounter them in such literature (as you often will) try substituting *Nous*, which is the Greek Hermetic term for Higher Mind, or use the term "Greater Force." 3) Approach your selected book as if encountering this philosophy for the first time. Even catching a single idea and being influenced by it could produce a ripple of change.

DAY 29
WHY NOT TODAY?

I woke up this morning not knowing what to post—I will never feed you generalities or invent some "insight" or homily to suit the hour. But it did occur to me: aiming for greatness is no larger or smaller than aiming for ordinariness. Today, I ask you to aspire within, and follow-up without, to utter excellence. Why couldn't this be the greatest day of your life as measured by reversing a depleting pattern, overcoming a chronic self-limitation, usurping a weakness, or pursuing the one "yes" that you need? (When seeking a solution, I always say: it takes only one yes.) There is no ethical or practical reason why not. Just as life visits catastrophes on us—often cultivated by habit—it also visits absurdly good news. This is as much a law of life as seasonal changes. Modernism has instilled us with the under-examined concept that life is intrinsically dark (e.g., Bertolt Brecht, Samuel Beckett). This is just a point of view. William James and Colin Wilson have suggested that generativity rather than depletion may be the governing law of life. In his 1895 essay, "Is Life Worth Living?", James addressed a wave of suicides among young men in America in the mid-1890s. He posited alternatives to suicide. One of the things he asked is whether the despairing person could stand it for just 24 hours longer. This is no trite observation. Twenty-four hours can bring revolutions. We live by leaps of assumption. The believer assumes; the agnostic or atheist assumes. As our experiment today, let us believe the highest of ourselves. On this, our second-to-last day, see what occurs.

DAY 30
HAPPINESS

I can hardly believe I am writing these words: welcome to Day 30 of the #30daymentalchallenge. It's not over—we have a full day ahead of us. What is happiness? It's impossible to be happy without physical and material security, so that is an inarguable baseline. Beyond that, I venture that happiness is *expressed selfhood*. We seek the establishment of self in our work, art, relationships, households, and so on. The manner in which selfhood is exercised or frustrated determines, more than any single factor, someone's happiness. "The mind is its own place," says John Milton's Dread Emperor, "and can make a heaven of hell and a hell of heaven." I bow to that statement. A similar precept resounds throughout New Thought literature, a literature unashamedly dedicated to happiness. But it resounds with a deficit, in my view. The positive-mind movement has culturally and theologically prescribed a certain kind of personality from which to view life. It is a personality defined by a "see no evil" gauziness. But what if that's not reflective of your nature? And if not, then you cannot be truly happy—or find a workable model—under its imperative. I see no reason to suppose that we all possess a convergent personality, one that dissolves into numinous serenity. Today I ask that you take seriously enough the dictum "know thyself" to really throw away whatever decisions someone else (or some tradition) has made about what defines you and your right perspective. You know the naturalness of right functioning. I know you know it. Because no life is exceptional and hence, sensitive people relate to each other's verities and struggles. When living from that place of individual naturalness, the mind becomes the creative tool that we feel it to be.

Thank you all so much for joining this 30-day effort. It continues always.

APPENDIX A
THE FULL TESTIMONY

In their 1931 book *Body, Mind, and Spirit*, ministers Elwood Worcester and Samuel McComb recount how a prominent scientist, who the authors do not name, told a small audience about how he dramatically improved his life through a one-month thought experiment. The account formed the basis of *The 30-Day Mental Challenge*. Chapter VII, "Suggestion," written by Worcester, introduced the man's testimony, called a "Striking Example," in this way: "Last spring I was present at a small gathering of men and women interested in medical psychology, to listen to an address by a famous man of science. After he had finished his formal talk, he said, in effect":

Ladies and gentlemen, before I sit down I wish to make a more personal statement which I think you will find of greater value and interest than my lecture. Up to my fiftieth year (he is now about sixty-five) I was an unhappy, ineffective man. None of the works on which my reputation rests was published. I was making my home in an unimportant town in California and was utterly unknown in the scientific world. I lived in a constant sense of gloom and failure. Perhaps my most painful symptom was a blinding headache, which recurred usually two days of the week, during which I could do nothing.

As my fiftieth birthday approached, I began to take stock of my soul and I realized that something was very wrong with me. I had read some of the literature of New Thought, which at the time appeared to be buncombe, and some statements of William James on the directing of attention to what is good and useful and ignoring the rest. One saying of his stuck in my mind, "We might have to give up our philosophy of evil, but what is that in comparison with gaining a life of goodness?" (or words to that effect).* Hitherto these doctrines had seemed to

---

* In his 1902 *The Varieties of Religious Experience*, James wrote, "Christian Science so-called, the sect of Mrs. Eddy, is the most radical branch of mind-cure in its dealings with evil. For it evil is simply a lie, and any one who mentions it is a liar. The optimistic ideal of duty forbids us to pay it

me only mystical theories, but realizing that my soul was sick and growing worse and that my life was intolerable, I determined to put them to the proof. In accordance with my teaching and mental habits, I resolved to make a careful, honest experiment which should be as carefully and honestly recorded. I decided to limit the period of conscious effort to one month, as I thought this time long enough to prove its value or its worthlessness to me. During this month I resolved to impose certain restrictions on my thoughts. If I thought of the past, I would try to let my mind dwell only on its happy, pleasing incidents, the bright days of my childhood, the inspiration of my teachers and the slow revelation of my life-work. In thinking of the present, I would deliberately turn my attention to its desirable elements, my home, the opportunities my solitude gave me to work, and so on, and I resolved to make the utmost use of these opportunities and to ignore the fact that they seemed to lead to nothing. In thinking of the future I determined to regard every worthy and

---

the compliment even of explicit attention. Of course, as our next lectures will show us, this is a bad speculative omission, but it is intimately linked with the practical merits of the system we are examining. Why regret a philosophy of evil, a mind-curer would ask us, if I can put you in possession of a life of good?"—MH

possible ambition as within my grasp. Ridiculous as this seemed at the time, in view of what has come to me since, I see that the only defect of my plan was that it aimed too low and did not include enough.

By this time I felt that I was about to make an important discovery and I began to be conscious of a certain tingling of expectation which I usually experience in my scientific work at such moments. When the day I had assigned arrived, I threw myself into the new task (incomparably the greatest I had ever attempted to perform) with ardor. I did not have to wait a month. At the end of eight days, I knew that the experiment was succeeding. I had not thought of including my headaches in my scheme of effort, as I deemed these beyond the possibility of help from this source. But therein I miscalculated, as they abruptly ceased. In fifteen years I have had but one headache and that was one I deliberately brought on for experimental purposes.

Apart from this welcome relief, the first change of which I was aware was that whereas for many years I had been profoundly unhappy, I now felt happy and contented. I knew what James meant when he spoke of "being consciously right and superior."* What surprised me more was that I was able to make others happy and that my personality seemed to attract, whereas before it had repelled. Up to this point of my recital I anticipate that you will find nothing strange in these changes and discoveries, except that I made them so late in life. What follows may tax your credulity. Personally I should not have accepted one of these statements sixteen years ago.

Yet most of the changes in my outer life are matters of fact, which can be verified in *Who's Who.* As I stated at the beginning, the burdens I found hardest to bear were my obscurity and isolation, consciousness that the passing years were bringing me no nearer the goal of my ambition, that although my capacity was considerable, my name was unknown and my works unpublished because no publisher would accept them.

---

* Again, in his 1902 *The Varieties of Religious Experience*, James wrote, "To be converted, to be regenerated, to receive grace, to experience religion, to gain an assurance, are so many phrases which denote the process, gradual or sudden, by which a self hitherto divided, and consciously wrong, inferior and unhappy, becomes unified and consciously right, superior and happy, in consequence of its firmer hold upon religious realities. This at least is what conversion signifies in general terms, whether or not we believe that a direct divine operation is needed to bring such a moral change about."—MH

The outward changes of my life resulting from my change of thought have surprised me more than the inward changes, yet they sprang from the latter. There were certain eminent men, for example, whose recognition I deeply craved. The foremost of these wrote me, out of a clear sky, and invited me to become his assistant. My works have all been published, and a foundation has been created to publish all that I may write in the future. The men with whom I have worked have been helpful and cooperative toward me chiefly on account of my changed disposition. Formerly they would not have endured me. One ambition of mine, my election to the presidency of a great foreign scientific society, though in accordance with my highest hope, seemed so utterly beyond my reach that I should have dreamed it preposterous to aim at it, yet it came to me. As I look back over all these changes, it seems to me that in some blind way I stumbled on a *path of life* and set forces to working for me which before were working against me.

There is one more incident I must record. After several years of peace and improvement it occurred to me that I had not given these theories a sufficient test. Apparently my experiment had succeeded, and I knew too much about the law of probability to ascribe all these changes to chance. Still, as a scientific man, I felt that I ought to test the principles with which I had been working negatively. I therefore began deliberately to revive the emotions of fear and apprehension. Within two hours I felt myself weak, depressed, doubtful, and I was conscious, for the last time, of a splitting headache. I therefore felt that I had done my duty and that I might rest comfortably in the great saying of Paul, "All things work together for good to them that love God."*

Worcester concluded, "If it were right for me to mention a great name, that of one of the least credulous or superstitious of mankind, this recital of his would evoke no mockery."

---

* This is from Romans 8:28 (King James Version): "And we know that all things work together for good to them that love God, to them who are the called according to his purpose."—MH

APPENDIX B
THE EMMANUEL MOVEMENT

The passage and source notes that follow are from my
One Simple Idea: How Positive Thinking Reshaped
Modern Life *(2014).*

In the wake of the medical licensing laws, the early
twentieth century was not a propitious moment for
religiously or psychologically oriented approaches
to medicine. Most physicians regarded any form
of positive-thinking or faith-based methods, even
when used as complementary treatments, as
smacking of Christian Science, a philosophy they
considered cultish and dangerous.* Protestant
churches took a similar view. While Catholicism
had long maintained a measured faith in healing
miracles and shrines, most Protestant seminaries

---

* I consider this summary judgment inadequate. I venture a much fuller
consideration of Christian Science in the book.—MH

and pulpits saw religious healing as something that had ended with the apostolic era.

Indeed, during the Reformation, Protestant movements often cast aspersions on the healing claims of the Catholic Church, considering talk of medical miracles as nothing more than the church's attempt to shore up its role as the exclusive organ of God's word on earth. That attitude more or less prevailed at the start of the twentieth century.

A few early twentieth century physicians grudgingly used bread pills or sugar remedies to placate hypochondriacal patients, and some doctors recognized the usefulness of hypnosis as an analgesic. But any talk of using mental or faith-based treatments was considered heresy in the medical community.

Richard C. Cabot, a young, Harvard-educated physician at Massachusetts General Hospital, had a different take.

Born in Brookline, Massachusetts, in 1868, Cabot, from his earliest years, inhaled the atmosphere of New England Transcendentalism. His father, James, was an intimate friend of Ralph Waldo Emerson's, to whom he served as editor, literary executor, and early biographer. The Cabot family attended a liberal Unitarian church, and

Richard studied at Harvard under William James and Idealist philosopher Josiah Royce.

William James was already devising the principles of the philosophy known as pragmatism. The heart of James's pragmatic outlook was that the measure of an idea's value was its effect on conduct. On this, James was uncompromising. To speak of allegiance to one creed or another was meaningless, he reasoned, unless you could demonstrate its impact on human behavior, "its cash-value, in terms of particular experience," he wrote in 1898.

Such thinking gave Cabot a framework for his own radical inquiries. He decided to become a medical doctor—but, crucially, he held to the belief that healing, like all facets of life, must be a composite. He believed that biologic cures in no way precluded, and often were aided by, the confidence of the patient, which could be fortified by faith, suggestion, and realistic, healthful self-belief. Taking a leaf from James's pragmatism, Cabot insisted that if a method healed, it was valid, whether the treatment was allopathic, alternative, spiritual, emotional, or any combination. While Cabot firmly believed that "spiritual healings" were really mental in nature, he conceded that the faculties at work were sometimes inscrutable and warranted further study.

"It is a thousand pities that these dissensions—these sectarian dissensions—have occurred in medicine as well as in religion," Cabot wrote in 1908. "We ought to get together. There is truth in all the schools; indeed there is nothing more characteristic of the American spirit than the realization of that fact."

Cabot was a brilliant laboratory researcher—at age twenty-eight in 1896 he wrote the first English-language textbook on hematology. Yet he turned down an opportunity to become the first bacteriologist at Massachusetts General Hospital; two years later he accepted a less prestigious position in the outpatient department. Cabot was more interested in face-to-face treatment than in lab research. He believed that physicians were assuming an inappropriately distant and inflated role in the new century, and were neglecting the experience, emotions, social problems, and fears of the patient. In response, Cabot hired the nation's first medical social worker at Massachusetts General in 1905. The hospital administration disapproved of the move and refused to pay her. Cabot paid the salary himself.

The following year, Cabot joined forces with a controversial and intriguing healing program, which emerged from an Episcopal church in Boston's Back Bay. Called the Emmanuel Movement, for Emmanuel Church which housed it, the project was a psycho-therapeutic clinic, presided over by the church's Reverend Elwood Worcester and his associate rector, Samuel McComb. The men sought to aid patients through prayer, support-group meetings, affirmations, hypnotic suggestion, and medical lectures delivered by Boston physicians.

The Emmanuel Movement sharply distanced itself from both Christian Science and mind-cure, insisting that its focus was limited to "functional nervous disorders," such as alcoholism, depression, migraines, chronic aches and pains, and digestive and bowel ailments. (This focus on "functional disorders" became a point of controversy, however, as the Emmanuel Movement also treated patients for tuberculosis, an infectious disease that then had no cure.) Further distinguishing itself from the mind-cure field, the Emmanuel clinic would see patients only on the referral and diagnosis of a physician. Reverend Worcester framed the clinic's activities not as an alternative to medicine but as a complement. The Emmanuel group received enormous, and often positive, media exposure, frequently from the nation's largest magazines, such as *Ladies' Home Journal* and *Good Housekeeping.*

Cabot became the Emmanuel Movement's chief medical advisor in 1906. He was intrigued not only by the relief that its methods seemed to bring, but by how the movement addressed a large number of ailments that, while real enough, didn't necessarily belong in the physician's examination room. "Now, without trying to limit the field precisely," Cabot wrote in 1908, "I should say that the diseases which are essentially mental or moral or spiritual in their origin should be treated (in part at least) by mental, moral and spiritual agencies. Cases of this type constitute in my experience about two-fifths of all the cases that come to an ordinary physician..." To Cabot the complementary approach was suited to disorders such as insomnia, digestive and bowel problems, and phantom aches and pains.

He felt, furthermore, that American medicine blinded itself with its specialized divisions. Every healer, from an osteopath to an allopath to a Christian Science practitioner, could speak of cure rates for those diseases that came to them, but not to the field of ailments in general. As Cabot saw it, medical professionals' frame of reference was too narrow, their willingness to collaborate too limited. Share patients and share data, he urged.

While Cabot believed in the efficacy of faith-based or mind-cure treatments, his support rested upon a strict distinction between "functional" and "organic" ailments. The mind-healing movements, he insisted, were highly capable of treating the kinds of functional diseases seen at the Emmanuel program—that is, bodily discomfort and stress-related disorders—which were not bacterial or structural. However, organic disease—biologic and organ-centered disorders—absolutely required standard medical care.

"Our friends the Christian Scientists," he wrote, "entirely ignore the distinction between organic and functional disease. I believe that organic disease is not helped to any extent by mental means, while functional disease has been helped a great deal by this means. Hence, there is nothing more important than to make clear this distinction."

Cabot's reasoning squares with the findings of today's most well-regarded placebo studies. The director of Harvard's Program in Placebo Studies and the Therapeutic Encounter, Ted J. Kaptchuk, told the *Wall Street Journal* in 2012: "Right now, I think evidence is that placebo changes not the underlying biology of an illness, but the way a person experiences or reacts to an illness." (It should be noted that Cabot considered placebos deceptive and he explicitly opposed their use; Kaptchuk's contemporary research, by contrast, centers on "transparent placebos," in which a patient knows he is receiving an inert substance. Kaptchuk's studies are considered later.)

For all the possibilities, Cabot and the Emmanuel Movement had limited success in winning the support of mainstream medicine. Cabot produced case studies and statistics showing traceable benefits from the Emmanuel program of prayer, encouragement, and religious counseling. Most medical professionals, however, turned up their noses. In journals and talks, physicians often complained that Emmanuel conflated the activities of doctors and clergy, and confused the public. (Cabot himself was never fully satisfied with the completeness of Emmanuel's record keeping.) "The Emmanuel movement," wrote physician Charles Dean Young in 1909 in the *Boston Medical and Surgical Journal*, "was and is, unquestionably well meant"—mental and spiritual healers had by this time come to realize that praise for good intent lined the steps to the guillotine—"but its originators are powerless to confine it within its legitimate bounds as the medical profession is powerless to prevent quackery, and, for some reason, the dear public does so love to be humbugged."

That same year Sigmund Freud visited America and, while he acknowledged knowing little about Emmanuel, the psychoanalyst told the *Boston Evening Transcript* on September 11: "This undertaking of a few men without medical, or with very superficial medical training, seems to me at the very least of questionable good. I can easily understand that this combination of church and psychotherapy appeals to the public, for the public has always had a certain weakness for everything that savors of mysteries . . . "

Ironically, the Emmanuel Movement, and other early strains of mind-cure, whetted the American appetite for Freud's theories of the unconscious. William James, who had contemporaneously labored to track the existence of a "subliminal mind," was dismayed by Freud's certainty that his psychoanalytic movement alone had science at its back. James wrote a colleague on September 28 that Freud had "condemned the American religious therapy (which has such extensive results) as very 'dangerous because so unscientific.' Bah!"

The controversies were no help to Cabot's career. In 1912, in what must have been a significant personal disappointment, Cabot was passed over for his expected appointment as Harvard's Jackson Professor of Medicine, one of the university's oldest medical professorships. Harvard instead opted for a professor who was more active in laboratory science. Cabot continued an important medical career, including as a director of battlefield medicine in France during World War I.

Following the war, Cabot launched a new campaign to urge American seminaries to train clergy in clinical and patient counseling. In 1925 he partnered with Anton Boisen, a minister who recovered following his institutionalization in a mental hospital to become one of the most eloquent voices for training seminary students in pastoral therapy. Cabot and his supporters met with measured success, helping to start pastoral training programs at Massachusetts General Hospital and Worcester State Hospital.

While widely copied in its early years, the Emmanuel Movement reached its end in 1929 with Reverend Worcester's retirement. There were no ready successors to his leadership. Indeed, none of Emmanuel's imitators were active for more than a few years. Emmanuel and its offshoots had petered out for reasons foreseen by Cabot: Ambitious clergy may have been willing to assume a counseling role, but they lacked training to sustain rigorous, ongoing programs. "The average clergyman," wrote Carl J. Scherzer, a hospital chaplain who had studied Emmanuel, "was not academically trained to undertake such a healing program even though he possessed a personality that might predict a reasonable amount of success in it."

Cabot died in 1939, ten years after Emmanuel closed its doors.

Although Cabot and Emmanuel failed to win over mainstream physicians, the movement proved a greater impact on the churches themselves. In a national survey of liberal Protestant ministers in the early 1950s, more than one-third of respondents reported using methods of spiritual healing, which included affirmations, individual and group prayer, and acts of forgiveness—all elements of the Emmanuel program. This was a marked change from Protestant clergy's indifference toward such measures at the start of the century. And Cabot's calls for pastoral clinical training found new champions in the next generation.

NOTES ON SOURCES

On the career of Richard C. Cabot, I benefited from Ian S. Evison's doctoral dissertation, *Pragmatism and Idealism in the Professions: The Case of Richard Clarke Cabot* (University of Chicago Divinity School, 1995). In an age when academic specialization has sequestered too much scholarship behind inscrutable terminology and ever-narrowing topic areas (trends that Cabot himself foresaw), Evison's study is a marvel of clarity across a wide breadth of subjects. Also of significant help were "The Conceptual Underpinnings of Social Work in Health Care" by Sarah Gehlert from *Handbook of Health Social Work* edited by Sarah Gehlert and Teri Arthur Browne (John Wiley & Sons, 2006); "The Emmanuel Movement, 1906–1929," by John Gardner Greene, *New England Quarterly,* September 1934; "'A Bold Plunge into the Sea of Values'; The Career of Dr. Richard Cabot" by Laurie O'Brien, *New England Quarterly,* vol. 58, no. 4, December 1985; "Richard Cabot: Medical Reformer During the Progressive Era" by T. Andrew Dodds, M.D., M.P.H., *Annals of Internal Medicine,* September 1, 1993; and "Clinical Pastoral Education" by Rodney J. R. Stokoe, *Nova Scotia Medical Bulletin,* vol. 53, 1974. William James's statement on the "cash-value" of an idea is from his "Philosophical Conceptions and Practical Results," *University Chronicle,* vol. 1, no. 4, September 1898. James's article is the text of a talk he delivered on August 28, 1898, at the Philosophical Union of UC Berkeley, where he outlined his philosophy of pragmatism; the event is worthy of a book in itself. Cabot's statement on "a thousand pities" is from Evison (1995). Cabot's statements on "moral or spiritual" diseases, and his passage on "functional" versus "organic" disease, are from his *Psychotherapy and Its Relation to Religion* (Moffat, Yard & Company, 1908). Cabot's book was one of a series of titles on medicine and religion published as a project of the Emmanuel Movement. Ted Kaptchuk is quoted from "Why Placebos Work Wonders" by Shirley S. Wang, *Wall Street Journal*, January 3, 2012. Charles Dean Young is quoted from his article "The Emmanuel Movement," *Boston Medical and Surgical Journal*, February 18, 1909. Both Freud and William James are quoted from Nathan G. Hale's *Freud and the Americans* (Oxford University Press, 1971). Peter D. Kramer is quoted from his *Freud: Inventor of the Modern Mind* (HarperCollins, 2006). On Cabot's advocacy of pastoral clinical training, I benefited from Stokoe (1974) and from the outstanding dissertation *From Jewish Science to Rabbinical Counseling: The Evaluation of the Relationship Between Religion and Health by the American Reform Rabbinate, 1916–1954,* by Rebecca Trachtenberg Alpert (Department of Philosophy, Temple University, 1978). Carl J. Scherzer is quoted from his article, "The

Emmanuel Movement," *Pastoral Psychology*, vol. 2, no. 11, February 1951. The survey of healing practices among Protestant ministers is detailed in Charles S. Braden's "Study of Spiritual Healing in the Churches," *Pastoral Psychology*, May 1954.

APPENDIX C
THE MAN WHO HELPED THE BEATLES ADMIT IT'S GETTING BETTER

THE TECHNIQUES OF FORGOTTEN MIND PIONEER EMILE COUÉ ARE SIMPLE, BUT THEY WORK

I originally wrote this piece for Medium *on June 10, 2019.*

One of the most significant names in modern psychological and motivational philosophy will evince blank looks from most people today: French mind theorist Emile Coué (1857–1926). Yet Coué, who earned both adulation and jeers during his lifetime, devised a simple, mantra-based method of self-reprogramming that has recently been validated across a wide range of disciplines, often by researchers who are unaware of the inceptive insights upon which their studies rest. I believe that Coué's methods not only deserve new credit and respect, but also hold promise for anyone in pursuit of practical therapeutic methods.

Coué proposed a simple formula of using mantras or affirmations to reprogram your psyche along the lines of confidence, enthusiasm, and wellness. His methods prefigured the work of self-help giants like Napoleon Hill, Maxwell Maltz, and Anthony Robbins, as well as recent clinical developments in sleep, neurological, placebo, and psychical research.

Indeed, at one time, thousands of people in the U.S. and Europe swore by Coué's approach. His key mantra—"Day by day, in every way, I am getting better and better"—was repeated by the Beatles, along with a wide range of therapists and spiritual writers. In rediscovering Coué, you will be able to determine for yourself if his simple approach works. Best of all, it requires only seconds each day.

THE BIRTH OF AN IDEA

Before exploring Coué's method and its application, it is useful to understand his unusual background. Born in Brittany in 1857, Emile Coué developed an early interest in hypnotism, which he pursued through a mail-order course from Rochester, New York. Coué studied hypnotic methods more rigorously in the late 1880s with French physician and therapist Ambroise-Auguste Liébeault. Liébeault was one of the founders of the so-called "Nancy School" of hypnotism, which promoted hypnotism's therapeutic uses. Leaving behind concepts of occultism and cosmic laws, many of the Nancy School hypnotists saw their treatment as a practical form of suggestion, mental reprogramming, relaxation, and psychotherapy.

This was Coué's view, bolstered by personal experience. While working in the early 1900s as a pharmacist in Troyes, in northwestern France, Coué made a startling discovery: Patients responded better to medications when he spoke in praise of the formula. Coué came to believe that the imagination aided not only recovery but also a person's general sense of well-being. From this insight, Coué developed his method of "conscious autosuggestion." This was essentially a form of waking hypnosis that involved repeating confidence-building mantras in a relaxed or semi-conscious state.

Coué argued that many of us suffer from poor self-image. This becomes unconsciously reinforced because your willpower, or drive to achieve, is overcome by your imagination, by which he meant one's habitual self-perceptions. In 1922 he wrote in *Self-Mastery Through Conscious Autosuggestion*, "When the will and the imagination are opposed to each other, it is always the imagination which wins." By way of example, he asked readers to think of walking across a wooden plank laid on the floor—obviously an easy task. But if the same plank is elevated high off the ground, the task becomes fraught with fear, even though the physical demand remains the same. This, Coué asserted, is what we are constantly doing on a mental level when we imagine ourselves as worthless or weak.

These insights are what drove the autosuggestion pioneer toward his signature achievement. Coué believed that through the power of self-suggestion or autosuggestion, any individual, with nearly any problem, could self-induce the same kinds of positive results he had observed when working in Troyes. In pursuit of an overarching method, Coué devised his self-affirming mantra: "Day by day, in every way, I am getting better and better." Although few people today have heard of Coué, many still recognize his formula. The mind theorist made his signature phrase famous through lecture tours of Europe and the U.S. in the early 1920s.

To critics, however, Coué reflected everything that was fickle and unsound about modern mind metaphysics and motivational philosophies. "How," they wondered, "could anyone believe that this little singsong mantra—'Day by day, in every way, I am getting better and better'—could solve anything?" But in a facet of Coué's career that is often overlooked, he demonstrated considerable insight, later validated by sleep researchers and others, into how he prescribed using the formula.

Coué explained that you must recite the "day by day" mantra just as you're drifting off to sleep at night when you're hovering within that very relaxed state between wakefulness and sleep. Sleep researchers now call these moments hypnagogia, an intriguing state of mind during which you possess sensory awareness, but your perceptions of reality bend and morph, like images from a Salvador Dalí painting. During hypnagogia, your mind is extremely supple and suggestible. Coué understood this by observation and deemed it the period to gently whisper to yourself 20 times: "Day by day, in every way, I am getting better and better." He didn't want you to rouse yourself from your near-sleep state by counting, so he recommended knotting a small string twenty times and then using this device like rosary beads to mark off your repetitions. He also said to repeat the same procedure at the very moment when you wake in the morning, which is a state sometimes called hypnopompia. It is similar to the nighttime state insofar as you are occupying a shadow world of consciousness yet possess sufficient cognition to direct your mental workings.

TOO EASY TO WORK?

Coué insisted that his mantra-based routine would reprogram your mind and uplift your abilities. Was he correct? There's one way to find out, at least for your own private purposes: Try it! We must never place ourselves above what are perceived by some as "simple" ideas. I have been influenced by the spiritual teacher Jiddu Krishnamurti (1895–1986), who emerged from the Vedic tradition but was an unclassifiable voice. Krishnamurti observed that the greatest impediment to self-development and independent thought is the wish for respectability. Nothing does more to stunt personal experiment, he taught, than the certainty that you must follow the compass point of accepted inquiry. Once you grow fixated on that compass point, nearly every-thing that you read, hear, and encounter gets eval-uated on whether it moves you closer to or further from its perceived direction. This makes independent experiment extremely difficult. But if you're unafraid of a little hands-on philosophy, Coué presents the perfect opportunity with his original mantra, intended to serve all purposes and circumstances. Of course, you can also craft your own simple mantra that reflects a specific desire, but you might want to start with Coué's original version to become comfortable with the practice.

If you need further encouragement to self-experiment, it may help you to realize that Coué's influence traveled in many remarkable directions. The Beatles tried Coué's method and apparently liked it, as references to Coué appear in some of their songs. In 1967, Paul McCartney used Coué's mantra in the infectious chorus of *Getting Better*, "It's getting better all the time . . . ," and the lyrics paid further tribute to the healer: "You gave me the word, I finally heard / I'm doing the best that I can." John Lennon also recited Coué's formula in his 1980 song *Beautiful Boy*, "Before you go to sleep, say a little prayer: Every day, in every way, it's getting better and better."

Beyond the Fab Four, placebo researchers at Harvard Medical School recently validated one of Coué's core insights. In January 2014, clinicians from Harvard's program in placebo studies published a paper reporting that migraine sufferers responded better to medication when given "positive information" about the drug.* This was the same observation Coué had made in the early 1900s. Harvard's study was considered a landmark because it suggested that the placebo response is always operative. It was the first study to use suggestion, in this case news about a drug's efficacy, in connection with an active drug rather than an inert substance, and hence, found that personal expectation impacts how, and to what extent, we experience an active drug's benefits. Although the Harvard paper echoed Coué's original insight, it made no mention of him.

I wondered whether the researchers had Coué in mind when they designed the study and asked one of the principals, who did not respond. So, I contacted the director of Harvard Medical School's program in placebo studies, Ted Kaptchuk, a remarkable and inquisitive clinician who also worked on the study. "Of course, I know about Coué," Kaptchuk told me, "'I'm getting better day by day.'" He agreed that the migraine study coalesced with Coué's observations, though the

---

* Kam-Hansen S, Jakubowski M, Kelley JM, Kirsch I, Hoaglin DC, Kaptchuk TJ, Burstein R; "Altered placebo and drug labeling changes the outcome of episodic migraine attacks," *Science Translational Medicine,* January 2014.

researchers had not been thinking of him when they designed it.

THE INFLUENCE OF AN IDEA

Coué's impact appears under the radar in an unusual range of places. An influential twentieth-century British Methodist minister named Leslie D. Weatherhead looked for a way that patients and seekers could effectively convince themselves of the truth and power of their affirmations, especially when such statements chafed against circumstantial reality, such as in cases of addiction or persistently low self-worth. Weatherhead was active in the Oxford Group in the 1930s, which preceded Alcoholics Anonymous in its pursuit of religious-therapeutic methods. In using suggestions or affirmations to improve one's sense of self-worth and puncture limiting beliefs, the minister was, in his own way, attempting to update the methods of Coué.

Weatherhead understood that affirmations—such as "I am confident and poised"—could not penetrate the "critical apparatus" of the human mind, which he compared to "a policeman on traffic duty." Other physicians and therapists similarly noted the problem of affirmations lacking emotional persuasiveness. Some therapists insisted that affirmations had to be credible in order to get through to the subject; no reasonable person would believe exaggerated self-claims, a point that Coué had also made. While Weatherhead agreed with these critiques, he also believed that the rational "traffic cop" could be eluded by two practices. The first was the act of repetition: "A policeman on duty who refuses, say, a cyclist the first time, might ultimately let him into the town if he presented himself again and again," he wrote in 1951. Continuing the metaphor, Weatherhead took matters further:

> I can imagine that a cyclist approaching a town might more easily elude the vigilance of a policeman if the attempt to do so were made in the half-light of early dawn or the dusk of evening. Here also the parable illumines a truth. The early morning, when we waken, and the evening, just as we drop off to sleep, are the best times for suggestions to be made to the mind.*

As Weatherhead saw it, the hypnagogic state— again, the drowsy state between wakefulness

---

* *Psychology, Religion, and Healing* (Abingdon-Cokesbury Press, 1951).

and sleep, generally experienced when a person is drifting off in the evening or coming to in the morning—is a period of unique psychological flexibility, when ordinary barriers are down. This is pure Couéism. Moreover, this fact probably reflects why people suffering from depression or anxiety report the early waking hours as the most difficult time of day—the rational defenses are slackened. If the individual could use the gentlest efforts to repeat affirmations, without rousing himself fully to a waking state, the new ideas could penetrate, Coué and Weatherhead believed.

The mystical writer Neville Goddard (1905–1972) made a similar point about the malleability of the hypnagogic mind. So did the 20th-century psychical researcher and scientist Charles Honorton (1946–1992), who used this observation as a basis for testing the potential for telepathy between individuals. Honorton believed that a hypnagogic state was, in effect, "prime time" for the reception of extrasensory communication, or what is more commonly called ESP.

In the early 1970s, Honorton and his collaborators embarked on a long-running series of highly regarded parapsychology ("psi") experiments, known as the "ganzfeld" experiments (German for "whole field"). These trials were designed to induce a hypnagogic state in a "receiver." The subject was placed, seated or reclining, in a soft-lit or darkened room and fitted with eye covers and earphones to create a state of comfortable sensory deprivation or low-level stimulation (such as with a "white noise" machine). Seated in another room, a "sender" would attempt to telepathically convey an image to the receiver. After the sending period ended, the receiver was asked to select the correct image from among four—three images were decoys, establishing a chance hit-rate of 25%. Experimenters found that receivers consistently made higher-than-chance selections of the correct "sent" image. Honorton collaborated with avowed skeptic and research psychologist Ray Hyman in reviewing the data from a wide range of ganzfeld experiments. The psychical researcher and the skeptic jointly wrote: "We agree that there is an overall significant effect in this database that cannot be reasonably explained by selective reporting or multiple analysis."* Honorton added, "Moreover, we agree that the significant outcomes have been produced by a number of different investigators."

---

* Hyman, R., & Honorton, C. (1986), "A joint communiqué: The psi ganzfeld controversy," *Journal of Parapsychology, 50*(4), 351–364.

Hyman insisted that none of this was proof of psi, though he later acknowledged that, "Contemporary ganzfeld experiments display methodological and statistical sophistication well above previous parapsychological research. Despite better controls and careful use of statistical inference, the investigators seem to be getting significant results that do not appear to derive from the more obvious flaws of previous research."* Although serious psychical research has come under withering, and often unfair criticism in recent years, the ganzfeld experiments have remained relatively untouched—and their methodological basis is derived directly from the insights of Coué.

THREE SIMPLE STEPS

Coué's presence also emerges in popular literature. One of the most enduring and beguiling pieces of popular metaphysics on the American scene is a 28-page pamphlet called *It Works,* written in 1926 by a Chicago ad executive named Roy Herbert Jarrett, who went under the alias "R.H.J."

---

* Hyman, Ray. "Evaluation of the program on anomalous mental phenomena," *The Journal of Parapsychology,* vol. 59, no. 4, Dec. 1995, pp. 321+.

His widely used method is to write down and focus on your desires—first, you must clarify your need; second, write it down and think of it always; and third, tell no one what you are doing to maintain mental steadiness. Plain enough, perhaps, but the seeker's insights rested on the deeper aspects of Couéism.

In the early 1920s, Jarrett and many other Americans were thrilled by news of Coué's mantra. The "Miracle Man of France" briefly grew into an international sensation as American newspapers featured *Ripley's-Believe-It-Or-Not*-styled drawings of Coué, looking like a goateed magician and gently displaying his knotted string at eye level like a hypnotic device. In early 1923, Coué embarked on a three-week lecture tour of America, with one of his final stops being Jarrett's hometown of Chicago, where the Frenchman spoke to a packed house at Orchestra Hall.

In a raucous scene, a crowd of more than 2,000 demanded that the therapist help a paralytic man who had been seated onstage. Coué defiantly told the audience that his autosuggestive treatments could work only on illnesses that originated in the mind. "I have not the magic hand," he insisted. Nonetheless, Coué approached the man and told him to concentrate on his legs and to repeat, "It is passing, it is passing." The seated man struggled up, haltingly walked, and the crowd exploded.* Coué rejected any notion that his "cure" was miraculous and insisted that the man's disease must have been psychosomatic.

To some Americans, Coué's message of self-affirmation held special relevance for oppressed people. The pages of Marcus Garvey's newspaper, *Negro World,* echoed Coué's "day by day" mantra in an editorial headline: "Every Day in Every Way We See Drawing Nearer and Nearer the Coming of the Dawn for Black Men." The paper editorialized that Marcus Garvey's teachings provided the same "uplifting psychic influence" as Coué's.**

Coué took a special liking to Americans. He found American attitudes a refreshing departure from what he knew back home. "The French mind," he wrote in 1923 in *My Method, including American Impressions*, "prefers first to discuss and argue on the fundamentals of a principle before inquiring into its practical adaptability to everyday

---

* "Crowd in Orchestra Hall Cheers Coué as His First Attempt in Chicago to Effect Cure Seems a Success," *Chicago Daily Tribune,* February 7, 1923. Also see "Youth's Tremors Quieted by Coué," *New York Times,* January 14, 1923, and "Emile Coué Dead, a Mental Healer," *New York Times,* July 3, 1926.

** The headline from Marcus Garvey's *Negro World* appeared September 15, 1923, and the editorial quote is from February 10, 1923

life. The American mind, on the contrary, immediately sees the possibilities of it, and seeks . . . to carry the idea further even than the author of it may have conceived."

The therapist could have been describing salesman-seeker Roy Herbert Jarrett and many others in the American positive-mind tradition. "A short while ago," Jarrett wrote in *It Works* in 1926, the year of Coué's death, "Dr. Emil [sic] Coué came to this country and showed thousands of people how to help themselves. Thousands of others spoofed at the idea, refused his assistance, and are today where they were before his visit."

Just as Coué had observed about the American mind, Jarrett sought to boldly expand on the uses of autosuggestion. Sounding the keynote of the American metaphysical tradition, Jarrett believed that subconscious-mind training did more than just recondition the mind: it activated a divine inner power that served to out-picture a person's mental images into the surrounding world. "I call this power 'Emmanuel' (God in us)," Jarrett wrote. In essence, the entirety of American positive-mind metaphysics rests on Coué-style methods.

Coué's instincts spoke to the individual's most profound wish for self-help and personal empowerment. It is my observation, as both a historian and seeker, that some people across generations have experienced genuine help through his ideas. So, once more, I invite you to disregard doubt and expectations and to self-experiment with Coué's method. We all possess the private agency of personal experiment; indeed, it may be the area in life in which we are most free. Yet we often get so wrapped up in the possibilities of digital culture and the excitement of social media that we neglect the technology of thought, through which we may be able to significantly reform some aspect of ourselves and our surrounding world.

You may find that the ideas of this mind pioneer, a figure so under-recognized in today's culture, offer the very simplicity and effectiveness that you have been seeking.

* * *

For a brief but complete explanation of how to use the mantra, I am providing the words of Emile Coué himself from this 1922 book, *Self-Mastery Through Conscious Autosuggestion:*

How To Practice
Conscious Autosuggestion

Every morning on awakening and every evening as soon as you are in bed, close your eyes, and without fixing your attention in what you say, pronounce twenty times, just loud enough so that you may hear your own words, the following phrase, using a string with twenty knots in it for counting: "DAY BY DAY, IN EVERY WAY, I AM GETTING BETTER AND BETTER."

The words: "IN EVERY WAY" being good for anything and everything, it is not necessary to formulate particular autosuggestions.

Make this autosuggestion with faith and confidence, and with the certainty that you are going to obtain what you desire.

Moreover, if during the day or night, you have a physical or mental pain or depression, immediately affirm to yourself that you are not going to CONSCIOUSLY contribute anything to maintain the pain or depression, but that it will disappear quickly. Then isolate yourself as much as possible, close your eyes, and pass your hand across your forehead, if your trouble is mental, or over the aching part of your body if physical, and repeat quickly, moving your lips, the words: "IT PASSES, IT PASSES," etc. Continue this as long as may be necessary, until the mental or physical pain has disappeared, which it usually does within twenty or twenty-

five seconds. Begin again every time you find it necessary to do so.

Like the first autosuggestion given above, you must repeat this one also with absolute faith and confidence, but calmly, without effort. Repeat the formula as litanies are repeated in church.

HOW TO TALK ABOUT CONTENTIOUS ISSUES IN SCIENCE

ONE AUSTRALIAN RESEARCHER GOT IT

This piece is adapted from my book The Miracle Club *(2018).*

I honor the perspective of journalist Norman Cousins who wrote in *Anatomy of an Illness* in 1979: "Not every illness can be overcome. But many people allow illness to disfigure their lives more than it should. They cave in needlessly. They ignore and weaken whatever powers they have for standing erect."

Although I urge caution throughout this book, I do *not* discount the possibility of extraordinary—even miraculous—episodes of recovery pertaining to the mind. And when I write "mind" I use an open-ended definition. If the mind has extra-physical dimensions, if it goes beyond cognition and motor commands, which I argue that it does, then the mind opens onto vistas that the human search, while millennia old, has only begun to detect.

Since the mid-1960s, a handful of physicians and clinicians have been making an effort to document one of the most astounding yet verifiable facts in the field of cancer research: spontaneous remissions of terminal cases.* In researching this question at the New York Academy of Medicine library, I found that about twenty such cases appear in world medical literature each year.** Many cases, clinicians agree, are probably unreported.

Based on estimated spontaneous regression rates worldwide—about one out of every one hundred thousand cases of cancer***—it can be extrapolated from the number of new cancer cases reported annually in the United States that about fifteen episodes of spontaneous regression occur

---

* See *Spontaneous Regression of Cancer* by T. C. Everson and W. H. Cole (W. B. Saunders, 1966).

** "The Spontaneous Regression of Cancer: A Review of Cases from 1900 to 1987" by G. B. Challis and H. J. Stam, *Acta Oncologica* 29, Fasc. 5 (1990).

*** "The Spontaneous Regression of Cancer: A Review of Cases," Challis and Stam.

here each year. There is no consensus around the causes of spontaneous remissions. Clinicians hypothesize that in rare cases patients may have been misdiagnosed, or patients may have been suffering from a severely impaired immune system, which, for reasons unknown, was restored to normal or exceptional functioning, perhaps due to the healing of an undetected virus or infection. Clinicians also acknowledge the possibility of mental therapeutics.

"Of all possible mechanisms cited for regression," wrote G. B. Challis and H. J. Stam in the journal *Acta Oncologica* in 1990, "the psychological is the only category which is not clearly biological." In surveying the extant literature, these researchers found that "only three authors are primarily responsible for reports of regressions by psychological means in the scientific literature"—and only one, Australian psychiatrist and researcher Ainslie Meares, "provided sufficient information to be able to include the cases in our tables."

Ainslie Meares (1910–1986) presented a special case in point. In the 1970s and '80s, Meares oversaw and published research on the practice of intensive meditation by terminally diagnosed cancer patients for whom traditional treatments, such as chemotherapy, had been discontinued;

in other cases, he employed intensive meditation (sometimes three hours a day) with patients who had "advanced cancer" but were still undergoing treatment. He documented notable therapeutic episodes in both groups.

In a 1980 report on seventy-three patients who had advanced cancer,* Meares found that intensive meditation helped relieve pain, depression, and anxiety, and contributed to a more peaceful and dignified death when cases proved terminal. In addition, Meares wrote of cancer patients who undergo intensive meditation: "There is reason to expect a ten percent chance of quite remarkable slowing of the rate of growth of the tumour, and a ten percent chance of less marked but still significant slowing. The results indicate that patients with advanced cancer have a ten percent chance of regression of the growth."

Meares also documented a small, but not isolated, number of cases where terminally diagnosed patients spontaneously regressed while following a protocol of intensive meditation. In an article in *Australian Family Physician* in March 1981,** he

---

* "What Can the Cancer Patient Expect from Intensive Meditation?", *Australian Family Physician* (May 1980).

** "Regression of the Recurrence of Carcinoma of the Breast at Mastectomy Site Associated with Intensive Meditation."

described the case of a fifty-four- year-old married woman with two grown children who had recovered from breast cancer following meditation. When a mastectomy failed to check her cancer growth, the patient had refused chemotherapy and embarked on a program of anabolic steroid use and natural supplements (which Meares neither studied nor endorsed). She began to show healing after seeing Meares for meditation sessions each weekday for one month, using a technique of sitting still and experiencing her "essential being," as he described it, without concentration of any kind. (In general, Meares restricted his research to subjects who had seen him for at least twenty meditation sessions of one hour or more daily. Although he does not specify the length of time this fifty-four-year-old woman sat daily, some of his patients meditated up to three hours a day.) He wrote of her remission:

A single case, considered by itself, may not be very convincing. But if we consider the particular case in conjunction with other patients who have responded in similar fashion, the relationship of treatment and outcome becomes more clearly established. In other words, the present case is not an isolated incident. It is one of a

series of cases of regression of cancer following intensive meditation in some of which the
regression has been more complete than in
others.

I was informally describing all this one evening in
2016 to a research pathologist at Harvard Medical
School who specializes in breast cancer. I broached
the topic with him of these rare but documented
cases of spontaneous remission. Some cases, as
noted, are evidently autoimmune related; but we
also talked about the correlations with intensive
meditation. The researcher's response: "I have to
be objective. But I have noticed that patients who
display a positive attitude toward their treatment
tend to do better. My colleagues have noticed this
too. We don't know why that is."

It is difficult to write about this kind of subject, even inconclusively, because it tends to polar-
ize. Readers with New Age sympathies are apt
to seize upon such discussions as validation that
mind-body medicine, perhaps coupled with some
kind of detox program, represents the royal road
to health. Meares said no such thing, and he was
scrupulous, as any responsible researcher would
be, not to plant false hopes. Yet there is an equal
and opposite extreme, in which a physician or skep-

tic (usually a journalist) approaches such a discussion without a sense of proportionality, assuming that *any* such talk is akin to propagating groundless "miracles" or wishful thinking. (Indeed, after I had noted the Harvard researcher's remarks on social media, another research physician I know objected that we were entertaining rash conclusions; he missed our expressed intent to avoid conclusions or leading questions but rather to frame a discussion.)

I want to give the final word to Meares, because his tone and carefulness exhibit what is needed today in the body-mind-spirit and New Thought culture. He wrote this in "Cancer, Psychosomatic Illness, and Hysteria" in *The Lancet* of November 7, 1981:

> In medicine we no longer expect to find a single cause for a disease; rather we expect to find a multiplicity of factors, organic and psychological. It is not suggested that psychological reactions, either psychosomatic or hysterical, are a direct cause of cancer. But it seems likely that reactions resembling those of psychosomatic illness and conversion hysteria operate as causes of cancer, more so in some cases than in others, and that they operate in conjunction

with the known chemical, viral, and radiational causes of the disease.

This is, to me, the kind of voice our society needs to cultivate generally—in politics, spirituality, and medicine. It is the voice that sustains a question, which is the vantage point from which all new understanding is gained.

MY 30-DAY
MENTAL CHALLENGE